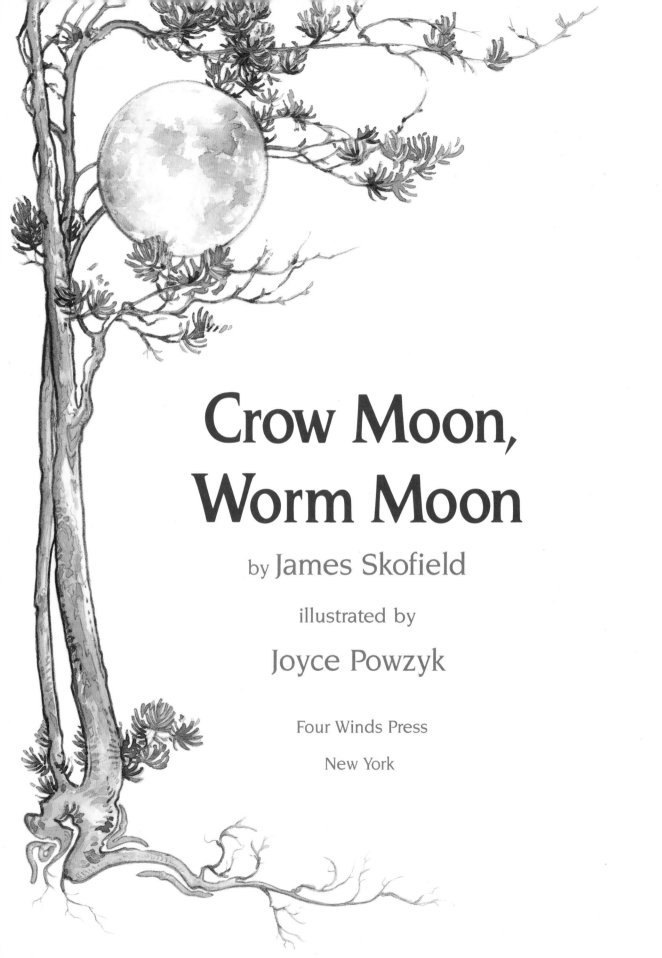

Crow Moon, Worm Moon

by James Skofield

illustrated by

Joyce Powzyk

Four Winds Press

New York

Four Winds Press, Macmillan Publishing Company
866 Third Avenue, New York, NY 10022
Collier Macmillan Canada, Inc.
Printed and bound in Hong Kong   First American Edition

10   9   8   7   6   5   4   3   2   1

The text of this book is set in 14 point ITC Novarese Book.
The illustrations are rendered in watercolor on rag paper.

Library of Congress Cataloging-in-Publication Data
Skofield, James. Crow Moon, Worm Moon / by James Skofield;
illustrated by Joyce Powzyk.—1st American ed.   p.   cm.
Summary: Plants and animals anticipate the arrival of spring in this
poem about the vernal equinox.
ISBN 0-02-782915-4
1. Moon—Juvenile poetry. 2. Children's poetry, American. [1. Spring—
Poetry. 2. Nature—Poetry.] I. Powzyk, Joyce Ann, ill. II. Title.
PS3569.K58C7   1990   811'.54—dc19
89-1370   CIP   AC

For Nina Shengold
and Jenifer Levin:
sisters & daughters
—J.S.

For Eleanor
—J.P.

Crow Moon and Worm Moon are terms used
to describe the full moon of the Vernal Equinox,
when day and night are of equal length and
winter gives way to spring. At this time of year,
the voices of crows change and their winter songs
become spring ones. Also, the earth has thawed
enough to allow hibernating worms to begin their
slow ascent to the surface of the ground.

Crow sings spring songs;
Crow sings low.
Crow sings in the dusk
to the woods below:

Moon over mountain,
Moon over water,
Moon on my shiny wings,
I am wind's daughter.

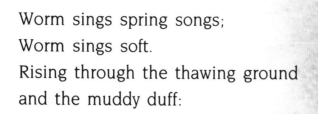

Worm sings spring songs;
Worm sings soft.
Rising through the thawing ground
and the muddy duff:

Moon over tangled roots,
Moon over water,
Moon wakes me from the chill,
I am earth's daughter.

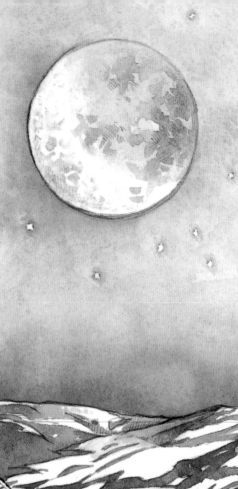

Sow bear stirs from sleep;
Sow bear yawns,
rumbles to her newborn cubs
in her winter den:

> Moon over hillside,
> Moon over water,
> Moon calls and I must forage
> for my sons and daughter.

Underneath the melting ice,
Trout swims and sculls.
Trout smells spring's scent
in the icy rills:

Moon over quiet pools,
Moon over water,
Moon on my silver scales,
I am river's daughter.

Maple sings spring songs.
Maple drinks deep;
strong green fire in her veins,
leaf buds curled in sleep:

Moon over forest,
Moon over water.
Wind, take my quickening seeds,
scatter sons and daughters.

Caterpillar rocking, drowsy,
in her spun cocoon,
wakes to find the spring moon flooding
through her silken room:

Moon over meadow,
Moon over water,
make me a butterfly,
light as a feather.

Moon sings spring songs;
Moon sings low.
Moon wakes the spring world
with her quiet glow:

Crow, in your nesting pine,
take your nesting slow;
soon your fine new eggs will hatch
and your fledglings grow.

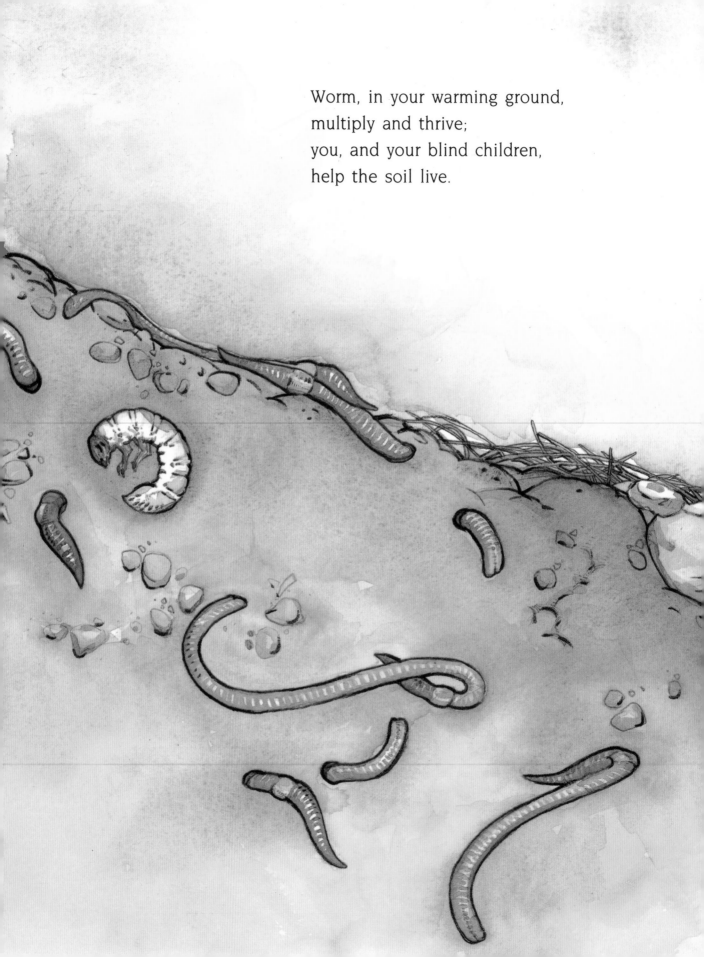

Worm, in your warming ground,
multiply and thrive;
you, and your blind children,
help the soil live.

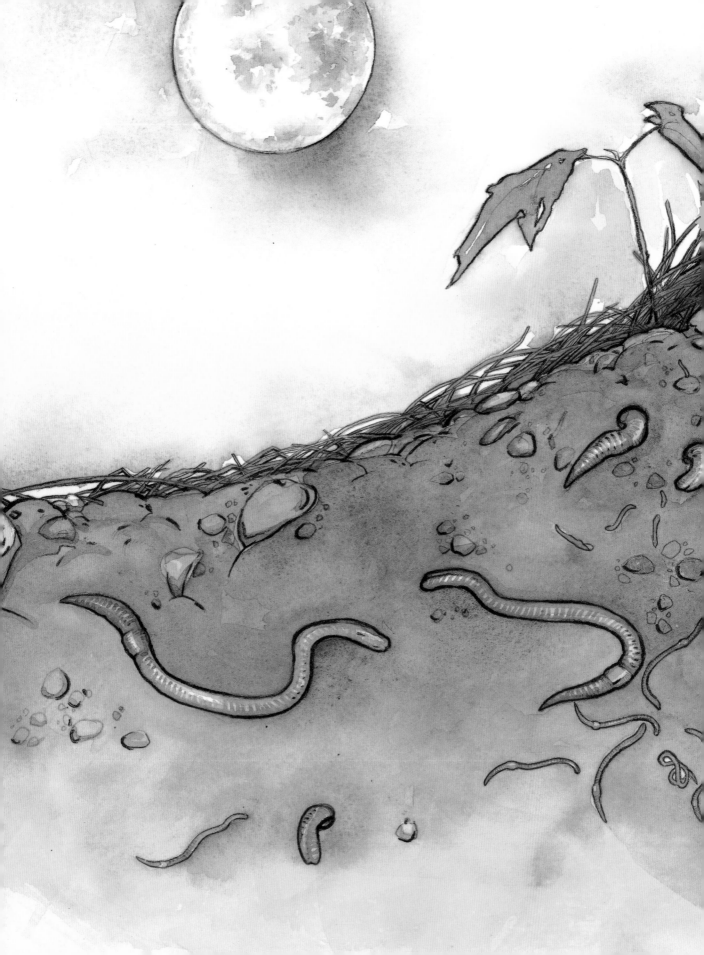

Sow bear, nurse your cubs
in your den of birth;
spring will lead to summer
and the bounties of the earth.

Trout, in your icy rill,
hear the call and spawn;
fingerlings will dart and feed
as the year flows on.

Maple, may your roots drink deep,
may your buds unfurl;
winged seeds will spread your children
far across the world.

Caterpillar, you shall dance
upon the summer air,
with wings as bright as soft moonlight
and finer than a hair.

Moon over mountain,
Moon over water,
wakens to spring
her wild daughters!